Date: 11/20/20

BR 597.34 SHA
Shaffer, Lindsay,
Whitetip reef sharks /

# Whitetip Reef Sharks

by Lindsay Shaffer

BLASTOFF! READERS
2

BELLWETHER MEDIA · MINNEAPOLIS, MN

Note to Librarians, Teachers, and Parents:

**Blastoff! Readers** are carefully developed by literacy experts and combine standards-based content with developmentally appropriate text.

**Level 1** provides the most support through repetition of high-frequency words, light text, predictable sentence patterns, and strong visual support.

**Level 2** offers early readers a bit more challenge through varied simple sentences, increased text load, and less repetition of high-frequency words.

**Level 3** advances early-fluent readers toward fluency through increased text and concept load, less reliance on visuals, longer sentences, and more literary language.

**Level 4** builds reading stamina by providing more text per page, increased use of punctuation, greater variation in sentence patterns, and increasingly challenging vocabulary.

**Level 5** encourages children to move from "learning to read" to "reading to learn" by providing even more text, varied writing styles, and less familiar topics.

Whichever book is right for your reader, Blastoff! Readers are the perfect books to build confidence and encourage a love of reading that will last a lifetime!

This edition first published in 2020 by Bellwether Media, Inc.

No part of this publication may be reproduced in whole or in part without written permission of the publisher. For information regarding permission, write to Bellwether Media, Inc., Attention: Permissions Department, 6012 Blue Circle Drive, Minnetonka, MN 55343.

Library of Congress Cataloging-in-Publication Data

Names: Shaffer, Lindsay, author.
Title: Whitetip Reef Sharks / by Lindsay Shaffer.
Description: Minneapolis, MN : Bellwether Media, Inc., 2020. | Series: Animals of the coral reef |
    Includes bibliographical references and index. | Audience: Ages 5-8 | Audience: Grades K-1 |
    Summary: "Relevant images match informative text in this introduction to whitetip reef sharks.
    Intended for students in kindergarten through third grade"--Provided by publisher.
Identifiers: LCCN 2019033047 (print) | LCCN 2019033048 (ebook) | ISBN
    9781644871362 (library binding) | ISBN 9781618918185 (ebook)
Subjects: LCSH: Oceanic whitetip shark--Juvenile literature.
Classification: LCC QL638.95.C3 S53 2020 (print) | LCC QL638.95.C3 (ebook) | DDC 597.3/4--dc23
LC record available at https://lccn.loc.gov/2019033047
LC ebook record available at https://lccn.loc.gov/2019033048

Editor: Betsy Rathburn    Designer: Laura Sowers

Printed in the United States of America, North Mankato, MN.

# Table of Contents

# Life in the Coral Reef

Whitetip reef sharks are found in warm ocean waters. Most live in coral reefs.

These sharks live well in the coral reef **biome**!

## Whitetip Reef Shark Range

N
W · E
S

range = ▭

5

Coral reefs are full of small tunnels and holes. Thin bodies help whitetips slip through these tight spaces.

Tough skin protects them
from sharp **corals**.

Whitetips have good **camouflage**. Pale bellies help them blend into sunlight from below.

tough skin

gray back

thin body

pale belly

From above, their gray backs blend into coral reef floors.

Whitetips have strong senses. They easily hear and smell **prey**.

Whitetips even sense heartbeats. These **adaptations** make them powerful hunters!

# Shark Caves

Coral reefs are busy places. Many creatures must share the space.

Whitetips cram together in caves. This keeps them safe from **predators**.

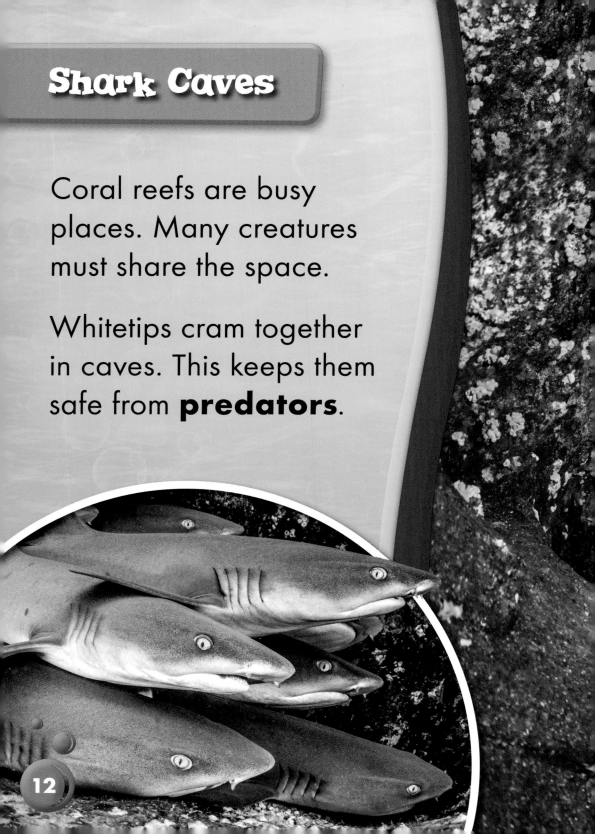

# Whitetip Reef Shark Stats

| Least Concern | Near Threatened | Vulnerable | Endangered | Critically Endangered | Extinct in the Wild | Extinct |
|---|---|---|---|---|---|---|

**conservation status: near threatened**

**life span: up to 25 years**

Coral reefs are full of **parasites**. They often feed on whitetips.

cleaner fish

The sharks stay near the floors of reefs. **Cleaner fish** eat parasites off their skin!

Whitetip reef sharks hunt
at night. They see well
in the dark.

They watch for the
movements of prey.
Then, whitetips attack!

Whitetips hunt along the ocean floor. They search cracks for hidden prey.

Eels and parrotfish
make tasty meals!

## Whitetip Reef Shark Diet

**banded
spiny lobsters**

**lagoon
triggerfish**

**steephead
parrotfish**

Whitetips sometimes hunt
in groups. They work together
to trap prey.

These sharks are powerful hunters in the coral reef biome!

# Glossary

**adaptations**—changes an animal undergoes over a long period of time to fit where it lives

**biome**—a large area with certain plants, animals, and weather

**camouflage**—coloring or markings that make animals look like their surroundings

**cleaner fish**—fish that remove parasites from coral reef animals

**corals**—the living ocean animals that build coral reefs

**parasites**—creatures that live on other living things and use them for food; parasites harm their hosts.

**predators**—animals that hunt other animals for food

**prey**—animals that are hunted by other animals for food

# To Learn More

**AT THE LIBRARY**

Hulick, Kathryn. *Coral Reefs.* New York, N.Y.: AV2 by Weigl, 2019.

Morey, Allan. *Hammerhead Sharks.* Mankato, Minn.: Amicus, 2017.

Schuetz, Kari. *Oceanic Whitetip Sharks and Pilot Fish.* Minneapolis, Minn.: Bellwether Media, 2019.

**ON THE WEB**

# FACTSURFER

Factsurfer.com gives you a safe, fun way to find more information.

1. Go to www.factsurfer.com.

2. Enter "whitetip reef sharks" into the search box and click 🔍.

3. Select your book cover to see a list of related web sites.

# Index

The images in this book are reproduced through the courtesy of: WaterFrame/ Alamy, front cover (whitetip reef shark); John_Walker, front cover (coral reef), pp. 2-3; Artyom Mirniy, pp. 4-5; Christine Wehrmeier/ Getty Images, p. 6; Krzysztof Bargiel, pp. 6-7; Tobias Bernhard Raff/ Biosphoto, pp. 8-9; Willyam Bradberry, pp. 9, 21; bradbclarke, pp. 10-11; Ethan Daniels, p. 11; Tomas Kotouc, p. 12; Martin Prochazkacz, pp. 12-13; wildestanimal/ Getty Images, p. 14; June Jacobsen, pp. 14-15; scubaluna, pp. 16-17; Jeffrey Rotman/ Biosphoto, p. 17; David Fleetham/ Alamy, pp. 18-19; Matt Haeger, p. 19 (lobsters); Vladimir Wrangel, p. 19 (triggerfish); Rich Carey, p. 19 (parrotfish); atese, pp. 20-21; abcphotosystem, p. 22.